BRISTOL
IN OLD PHOTOGRAPHS
FROM THE FRED LITTLE COLLECTION

FRED LITTLE – Born in 1875 in Bristol. He started his career in Narrow Wine Street, moving to Castle Mill Street in the early 1900s where the business was finally taken over in 1937. During his career, he became a well-known Bristol commercial photographer recording sights of Bristol to be used for the production of postcards. Fred died in 1953 aged 77.

BRISTOL
IN OLD PHOTOGRAPHS
FROM THE FRED LITTLE COLLECTION

COLLECTED BY
DELLA MOORCROFT &
NEIL CAMPBELL-SHARP

ALAN SUTTON
1988

Alan Sutton Publishing Limited
Brunswick Road · Gloucester

First published 1988

British Library Cataloguing in Publication Data

Bristol in old photographs.
1. Avon. Bristol, history
I. Campbell-Sharp, Neil   II. Moorcroft, Della
942.3'93

ISBN 0-86299-518-3

Typesetting and origination by
Alan Sutton Publishing Limited.
Printed in Great Britain by
WBC Print Limited

INTRODUCTION

More than a hundred years has elapsed since the first photographs in this virtually unique collection were taken, and just a brief glimpse at their content illustrates all too clearly the architectural cost of the Second World War and the changes caused by the city's expansion.

The collection chronicles life in Bristol leading up to and passing the turn of the century, and in an effort to help the reader I have collated the photographs in such a way as to lead one through Bristol in a logical way. In this manner the reader may compare the architecture and viewpoint and see the changes made in the past hundred years.

Having viewed Fred Little's collection so regularly over a period of time, I cannot but be impressed by the photographic techniques used to depict these visual scenes on a two dimensional plane. One can only marvel at the quality of these photographs even when compared with present-day work with technology like auto-exposure, autofocus and variable focal lenses.

I felt when this collection came into my possession that, as a keen photographer, I owed it to the originator of this beautiful work to collate and produce photographs of a quality that Fred Little would have been proud of. I hope that with the help of Neil Campbell-Sharp I have fulfilled this wish and that the people of Bristol will feel the same when viewing and reading this book.

I hope this collection will help to achieve the deserved accolade for Fred Little's perceptive photographs and to preserve for him this unique chronicle of Bristol history.

Della Moorcroft

A SOUVENIR OF BRISTOL – One of the many brochure covers Fred Little was commissioned to undertake.

THE STATUE OF NEPTUNE – Erected on 26 November 1872 on the junction of Temple and Victoria Street.

QUEEN VICTORIA STATUE – College Green. The Queen's statue was erected on College Green in 1887 to celebrate her Golden Jubilee.

QUEEN VICTORIA STATUE – 1899. The statue was unveiled on 25 July 1888 by HRH Prince Albert Victor, Duke of Clarence, the eldest son of the Prince of Wales. HRH arrived in Bristol at midday and was escorted to the Council House, where he was presented with the Freedom of the City. He then proceeded to College Green for the unveiling ceremony which was marred by heavy rain showers.

THE STATUE OF QUEEN VICTORIA situated on College Green.

THE CIVIC HIGH CROSS, College Green. This beautiful cross was a replica of the original which was erected at the intersection of High Street, Corn Street, Wine Street and Broad Street. It was at this spot that monarchs were proclaimed and traitors beheaded. The old cross was moved from its original site in 1768 to a new home in Stourhead where it stands today.

THE CIVIC HIGH CROSS. The original cross was erected in 1373 on the junction of High Street, Wine Street, Corn Street and Broad Street. It was removed in 1768 and given to Henry Hoare, a friend of the Dean of Bristol, who used it as a focal point in Stourhead. The replica, seen in this picture, was erected in 1850.

THE CIVIC HIGH CROSS. Carved at the top of this beautiful cross are the statues of the eight kings who honoured Bristol with their charters.

COLLEGE GREEN. The avenue of trees which once graced the Green. These were subsequently taken down to clear the site for the new Council House.

BRISTOL CATHEDRAL. Front view of the two west towers of Bristol Cathedral which was originally an Augustinian abbey founded in the twelfth century and built of local Dundry stone. The Norman chapter house dates back to 1142.

BRISTOL CATHEDRAL. Outside the cathedral, hansom cabs await their fares.

BRISTOL CATHEDRAL.

BRISTOL CATHEDRAL. The monument to Sir John and Lady Young was erected in 1606. Sir John was the son of a wealthy Bristol merchant. He was knighted by Queen Elizabeth in Bristol in 1574. Lady Young's family, the Wadhams, founded Wadham College in Oxford.

BRISTOL CATHEDRAL. Monument to Sir Charles Vaughan AD 1630.

INTERIOR OF BRISTOL CATHEDRAL. The north choir aisle.

BRISTOL CATHEDRAL. The eastern Lady Chapel, begun in 1298, forms an integral part of the design of the whole choir.

ONCE SITUATED NEAR THE CATHEDRAL, the Bishop's Palace was burned down during the Bristol Riots which began on Saturday 29 October 1831. The unrest was occasioned by the stormy parliamentary progress of the Electoral Reform Bill, of which Bristol's Bishop Gray was a well-known opponent. The riots were sparked off when, after the reading of the Riot Act, Dragoon Guards under the command of Colonel Brereton charged an unruly crowd of partisans of both political factions which had gathered in Queens Square. During the weekend of violence 500 rioters were killed, Colonel Brereton shot himself, the Bishop's Palace was destroyed by fire and books and documents from the Cathedral library were burned. Four of the rioters arrested during the fighting were hung and a further 88 transported to the colonies.

NORMAN GATE – DEANERY ROAD. This beautiful gateway adjoins the Central Library. It was once the Abbey gatehouse where pilgrims received the dole and drink.

CENTRAL LIBRARY – DEANERY ROAD. The beautiful carved fireplace by G. Gibbons.

PORT OF BRISTOL. A beautiful centrepiece for the Port of Bristol.

BRISTOL HARBOUR. A peaceful scene in Bristol Harbour showing the tall masted sailing ships.

BRISTOL HARBOUR. To the right of the picture you can see the cranes which were used for hoisting the heavy cargo from the deep holds of the sailing ships.

THE BRISTOL HARBOUR. Ships like this were once frequent visitors to Bristol Harbour.

BRISTOL HARBOUR. During the seventeenth century, ships like these sailed from Bristol laden with families and fortune hunters, all hoping to find a new way of life. As a result of their voyages, trade between Britain and the New World increased, bringing tobacco and sugar from Barbados, the West Indies and the Americas.

BRISTOL HARBOUR. Another beautiful scene looking towards the west of the Bristol floating harbour.

HOTWELLS LIBRARY. This fine old building once stood beside St Peters Church in Jacobs Wells Road.

CABOT TOWER – BRANDON HILL. This magnificent tower was designed by W.V. Gough and cost approximately £3,250 to build. It is shown here during its construction. The first stone was laid in 1897. Note the use of wooden scaffolding.

CABOT TOWER – BRANDON HILL. Standing 105 feet high and built of red rubble stone, this tower was opened on 6 September 1898. It was built to commemorate John Cabot's sailing in the 50-ton *Matthews* with a crew of 18 men from Bristol on 14 June 1497, and his discovery of Newfoundland.

CABOT TOWER – BRANDON HILL.

CABOT TOWER – BRANDON HILL.

VIEW FROM CABOT TOWER. From the foot of Cabot Tower there is a magnificent view of the city of Bristol with its many church spires.

VIEW FROM CABOT TOWER. One of the fine cannons which once stood at the foot of Cabot Tower.

OLD CITY MUSEUM. The City Museum until the Blitz, after which the frontage survived. This now fronts the University Refectory.

OLD ART GALLERY. This fine building has been used as the museum since the Blitz.

RED LODGE – PARK ROW. The fireplace in the Great Oak Room. Fireplaces like this one were prized possessions in the sixteenth century, when flueless hearths were still common.

ANOTHER FINE EXAMPLE of a beautiful sixteenth-century fireplace.

FINE CARVED CHAIRS which were once used in the Court Rooms.

BEAUTIFUL CHAIRS, one showing the beehive and the working bees; symbols used to show the hard work achieved in the Court Room.

THE OLD COURT ROOMS. A fine example of the carved doorways which were typical of this period.

REDWOOD LODGE.

PLASTER-MOULDED CEILINGS copied from the original wooden ceilings which enhanced the Bristol Mansions, many of which can be seen today.

BOER WAR MEMORIAL. This is a memorial to the men of the Gloucester Regiment who fell in the Boer War. People say that he is a disgrace to his Regiment as he is placing the wrong foot forward!

39

CLIFTON BRIDGE. Taken from Hotwells at 10.15 p.m. on 14 July 1908.

CLIFTON BRIDGE. Taken from Cumberland Basin. On the left is Rownham Ferry.

SION HILL. The Clifton entrance to the Clifton Bridge.

CLIFTON BRIDGE, 1916. Designed by Isambard Kingdom Brunel who won a competition run by the Merchant Venturers for the best design of bridge to span the Avon Gorge. The bridge was completed in 1864 after Brunel's death.

AVON GORGE. Scene taken from Shirehampton up the Gorge towards the Clifton Bridge.

S.S. *GYPSY* – 12 MAY 1878. The *Gypsy* was wrecked in the Avon Gorge, hitting the bank opposite the Gully. 200lb of dynamite was used to dislodge the ship.

RIVER AVON. Sailing ships up the Gorge. Bridge Valley Road leads up on the right.

CUMBERLAND BASIN – HOTWELLS. This was in the main entrance to the Floating Harbour. William Jessop had a fresh channel dug for the River Avon and dammed it, leaving the ships 'floating' between the tides. This view over the Basin was taken from Rownham Hill.

THE OBSERVATORY – CLIFTON. This observatory was built by William West in 1828 on the site of an old snuffmill which was burnt out in 1777. Mr West fitted a camera obscura in the top of the tower – a rotating cowl reflecting onto a table, showing a picture of 5ft in diameter. Situated 337 feet above sea level, the camera obscura showed the movement of people and the coming and going of ships below, in colour.

THE OBSERVATORY. Situated on the cliffs at the top of the Gorge, Mr West excavated a passage to 'Ghyston Cave', also known as 'Giants Cave', 90ft below. This cave is a natural cavern once used as a hermitage.

PROCTOR'S FOUNTAIN – BRIDGE VALLEY ROAD. The fountain was erected in 1872 to mark the gift of Clifton Down to Bristol citizens by the Society of Merchant Venturers.

THE QUEEN VICTORIA CONVALESCENT HOME.

MANSION HOUSE. Sited on the corner of Clifton Down Road and Canynage Road. The house was given to the city in 1874 by Alderman Proctor to replace the one in Queens Square destroyed in the Bristol Riots. This is the residence of the Lord Mayor and dates from 1867.

THE LORD MAYOR. Sir Herbert Ashman became the first Lord Mayor of Bristol in June 1899 and was knighted by Queen Victoria on the 15 November 1899. Queen Victoria was in Bristol to open the Convalescent Home on the Downs. The royal train from Windsor arrived at 2 o'clock and the procession passed along Victoria Street and on to the Council House in Corn Street whereupon the Queen commanded the Lord Mayor to kneel. When the Duke of Connaught provided her with a sword, she touched the Chief Magistrate on the shoulder and bade him rise as Sir Herbert Ashman. This was the last personal conferment of a knighthood by the Queen.

BRISTOL ZOO – CLIFTON DOWNS. Opened in 1836.

BRISTOL ZOO – CLIFTON DOWNS. People liked to dress up in their Sunday best for day trips to the Zoological Gardens. Note the hydrogen balloon tethered in the grounds.

CLIFTON DOWNS. View of the tidal River Avon.

Above right
WHITELADIES ROAD – 1878. The top of Whiteladies Road decorated for the royal visit on the 12 July 1878 of the Prince of Wales, who visited the City of Bristol Agricultural Show on Clifton Downs. The Prince arrived at Temple Meads station at 12.45 p.m. and was driven via High Street, Corn Street and College Green, along Whiteladies Road to the Downs. Thousands of people attended the show and there was the highest entry of cattle on record. The Prince of Wales left the Downs via the Suspension Bridge to Clifton Down station where a special train waited to take him to London.

WHITELADIES ROAD — 1878. Whiteladies Road at Blackboy Hill. This arch welcomed HRH to the show on Clifton Downs. The central span was 30ft wide and the two side arches each 20ft wide.

COLSTON'S ALMHOUSES – ST MICHAEL'S HILL. In 1695 Edmund Colston erected this almshouse for 12 men and 16 women, stating a preference for people who had lived in 'some sort of decency' rather than those who had had 'a vicious life' or were 'drunkards', as they would not make good neighbours.

BRISTOL ROYAL INFIRMARY, Marlborough Hill. Built in 1736 of Portland stone.

ST JAMES BARTON – LEWINS MEAD. The church nave became a parish church in 1374. It is all that remains of Bristol's earliest monastery. The original priory was erected in 1130 by Robert, Earl of Gloucester. It is said that for every 10 stones he imported from Normandy for the castle keep, he gave one stone for the building of this priory church.

ST JAMES BARTON – LEWINS MEAD.

ST JAMES CHURCH.

ST JAMES PARADE.

ST JAMES BARTON. An Adams fireplace.

LEWINS MEAD. The Horsefair.

ARLEY CHAPEL, Cheltenham Road. Consecrated in 1845, it is now the Polish Church.

GEORGE MÜLLER. Born in Prussia, the son of a tax collector, he survived a wayward youth of heavy drinking and dishonesty to become one of Bristol's greatest social reformers. He came to Bristol in 1832 and was appalled by the sight of children begging in the streets of the city. This prompted him to open an orphanage four years later in Wilson Street. He died, aged 92, in 1892.

MILK STREET – ST PAULS.

THE CHAPEL – LAWFORDS GATE PRISON, Old Market. The ghostly image of a man on the left of the picture is due to the long exposure needed to take this interior photograph.

THE WHIPPING POST – LAWFORDS GATE PRISON, Old Market. The prison was built in the 1790s and had 70 cells. The prisoners were all released by the mobs in the 1831 riots. It was disused in 1860.

THE COBBLER. These bootmakers worked from the Old Market and Kingswood area of the city, making and repairing boots for the miners.

OLD MARKET STREET. This was the site for the castle garrison in the thirteenth century.

OLD MARKET STREET. In the seventeenth century country people would set up their stalls and trade in the main street. It was the widest thoroughfare in Bristol.

OLD HOUSE – MERCHANT STREET. No. 22 – the locksmith Wm. Evans lived here. It was later demolished to make room for Quakers Friars.

ALMSHOUSES – OLD MARKET STREET.

STAR DINING ROOMS. 34 West Street, Old Market.

THE INTERIOR OF ALL HALLOWS CHURCH, Easton.

THE CHURCH OF ST PHILLIP & JACOB, built in 1193 as a country church. It was in a peaceful setting away from the crowded city.

ST PHILLIP & JACOB. The quiet churchyard of St Phillip & Jacob with its well-kept gardens. It is now known as 'Pip 'n' Jay'.

SLOPER'S LANE, OFF NARROW PLAIN.

THE SHAKESPEARE. The local newspaper – *Bristol Times & Mirror* – on sale outside this superb building in Victoria Street.

THE SHAKESPEARE. Built in 1636. The façade is original and has been preserved.

TEMPLE CHURCH. This church has a leaning tower of 113 feet high which is approximately five feet out of true. Building began in 1300, but the tower subsided when almost half complete and work was stopped for 60 years.

VICTORIA STREET. A bustling shopping thoroughfare. Note the garage on the right of the picture selling Daimler vehicles, but the almost complete absence of motorised vehicles elsewhere.

STATUE OF NEPTUNE. Cast by the Bristol founder John Rendall in 1723 and sited here on the junction of Victoria and Temple Street. At present it stands at the head of St Augustine's Reach in the city centre.

THE OLD INN. Thomas Street towards Mitchell Lane. This was originally one of the many coaching inns and was later used as an L & NWR parcels office as you can see from the signs.

THE THREE KINGS, Thomas Street.

THOMAS CHATTERTON'S MONUMENT. This statue was erected in memory of the boy poet Thomas Chatterton in 1840 near the north porch of St Mary Redcliffe. It was banished from consecrated ground in 1846. His father was Master at Redcliffe Charity School where Thomas attended, but died before Thomas was born. Thomas suffered from rejection by other poets – living on next to nothing – his pride finally beat him and he committed suicide at the age of 18.

INTERIOR OF ST MARY REDCLIFFE CHURCH.

ST JOHN'S HERMITAGE, Redcliffe Parade. This cave was lived in from 1346 to 1669 by a succession of anchorites. It is situated in the garden of Redcliffe Parade which dates back to 1665, when Charles II granted the plot to the Society of Friends as a burial ground.

BEDMINSTER PARADE. The Mayor's procession in Bedminster Parade – in the background was the building of W.D. & H.O. Wills with its prominent towers.

BEDMINSTER PARADE.

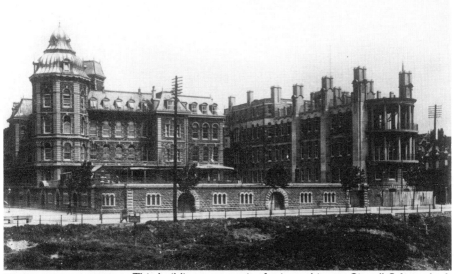

BRISTOL GENERAL HOSPITAL. This building won a prize for its architects, Gingell & Lysaght. It was built in 'Warehouse' style with the idea of constructing the basement to provide 8,000 square feet of warehouse space which could be let to merchants using the Bathurst Basin, and therefore providing an income for the hospital. It was built in 1853 to take care of all the casualties from the docks.

PRINCES STREET BRIDGE.

MERCHANT VENTURERS ALMSHOUSES, King Street. The Society of Merchant Venturers founded these residential almshouses for seamen in 1554. A coat of arms of the Society, including a mermaid with an anchor and Father Time, is depicted on the upper wall.

81

THE OLD LIBRARY, KING STREET.

THE OLD LIBRARY, KING STREET. The old staircase.

KING WILLIAM III, QUEEN'S SQUARE.

KING WILLIAM III, QUEEN'S SQUARE. Rysbrack's monument to William III was erected in 1736.

KING WILLIAM III, QUEEN'S SQUARE. Railings and a policeman protect the monument.

THE CITY CENTRE.

How THE CENTRE WILL Look, "IF WE GET much more RAIN" Bristol

THE CITY CENTRE. One of Fred's 'Little' jokes showing how the centre would look if we had much more rain!

THE DRAWBRIDGE in 1908. The city centre from St Augustine's Parade.

THE MERCHANTS' HALL – MARSH STREET. The HQ of the Society of Merchant Venturers. Built in 1720 and blitzed in 1940, it is now the site of the ring road leading to the Prince Street roundabout.

COLSTON'S STATUE. Unveiled in 1895, this statue was the work of Manchester sculptor John Cassidy and depicts Edward Colston as an old man. Edward Colston was founder of two schools and his almshouses. He gave over £70,000 to his native city.

EDMUND BURKE'S STATUE. Unveiled in 1894. Edmund Burke was an Anglo-Irish politician who was elected to represent Bristol in 1774. He lost his seat in 1780 because he supported proposals to relax restrictions on trade between Ireland and Britain.

STEEP STREET. Until 1871 Steep Street was the main road to Gloucester and the Aust Ferry. The steps on the left were changed from 14 to 17 steps in 1854 and a notice at the foot of the steps read 'It is an offence for anyone to deposit dirt or ashes' and a reward of 5s. was offered to persons giving information.

CHRISTMAS STREET. The foot of Christmas Steps. On the right is the entrance to St Bartholomew's thirteeth-century hospital, founded for sailors at some time before 1207.

OLD MERCHANT TRADE SCHOOL, Nelson Street. Established in 1856. The Society took over the management and finance of the Trade School in 1885 from Colston Trustees.

ST JOHN'S GATE. Queen Elizabeth I rode on a white horse through this gateway when she visited the city in 1574.

ST JOHN'S GATE. The carving of Belinus who, with his brother Brennus, the sons of a king in Britain, were said to have led a great army of Gauls into Italy and laid waste a huge part of that country, including Rome. Returning with their victories in 390 BC they founded the town of Bristol in the Valley of the Avon.

ST JOHN'S GATEWAY, leading to Broad Street.

TAYLORS COURT, off Broad Street. This seventeenth-century courtyard was granted to the Fraternity of Tailors to assemble on festival days, in their gowns, to meet the Mayor and transact the Fraternity's business.

ASSIZE COURTS. A beautiful carved fireplace.

ST JOHNS ARCH. Once a Norman gateway in part of the earliest town wall. The wall was 10ft thick.

ST JOHN'S ARCH, 21 March 1911 in Tower Lane. The start of the demolition.

ST JOHN'S ARCH – March 1911, Tower Lane.

ST JOHN'S ARCH, Tower Lane.

ST JOHN'S ARCH, Tower Lane, when demolished.

ST JOHN'S ARCH.

FAIRFAX STREET, opened in 1866.

FAIRFAX STREET. N. Morley & Sons, rag merchants trading in Fairfax Street.

THE ARCADE, Broadmead, built in 1824.

THE GREYHOUND. An old coaching house which still retains many of its links with the eighteenth century, including a 'Bristol Unicorn' Firemark.

MERCHANT STREET, 1889.

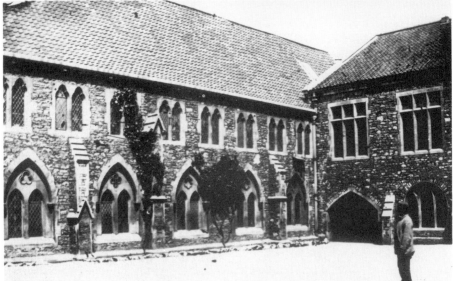

QUAKERS FRIARS, between Merchant and Penn Street – a Dominican friary that dates from 1230.

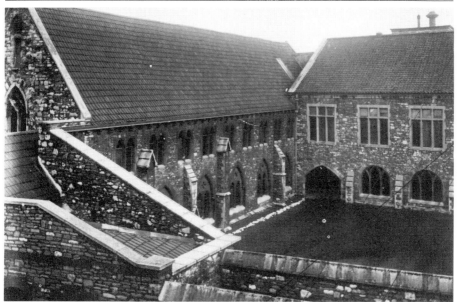

QUAKERS FRIARS. The Quakers were members of a religious sect which suffered great persecution in the early days of its existence. In 1670 the Quakers erected their first house in the ruins of the old Dominican friary.

QUAKERS FRIARS. The above buildings were constructed by George Tully in 1747.

A QUAKER FRIAR.

THE CAT & WHEEL, Castle Green, on the corner of Little Peter Street and Castle Green.

THE REMAINS OF BRISTOL CASTLE, Castle Green, destroyed 1911.

CASTLE STREET. A Sunday School between Tower Street and Cock & Bottle Lane.

ST PETER'S HOSPITAL, at the top of Castle Green, once stood behind St Peter's Church and was first mentioned in 1402. It was rebuilt in 1612 and became the Bristol Mint in 1695, then later still became a hospital for the sick poor. Unfortunately the hospital went up in flames in the Blitz.

A FINE CARVED FIREPLACE in St Peter's Hospital.

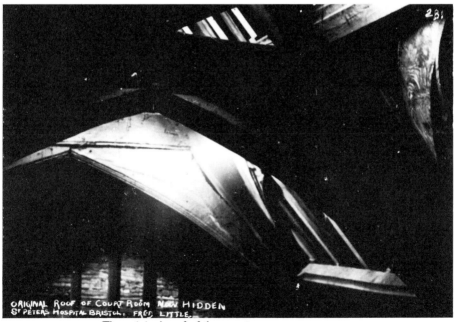

ST PETER'S HOSPITAL. The original roof of the court room.

HIGH STREET IN THE 1800s. In 1864 the Druids' Arms was demolished to widen St Nicholas Street and the Angel Inn collapsed.

ST PETER'S CHURCH ancient drapings.

CHURCH OF ST MARY LE PORT.

INTERIOR OF ST MARY LE PORT.

ST MARY LE PORT. The reredos and brass eagle lectern, dated 1683, were victims of the Blitz.

WINE STREET celebrating the royal visit.

WINE STREET. Note the horse-drawn carriage on the right.

ONE OF THE MANY BUILDINGS decorated for the royal visit.

WINE STREET. Jones & Co. retailing from the Guard House in Wine Street.

JONES & CO.

WINE STREET.

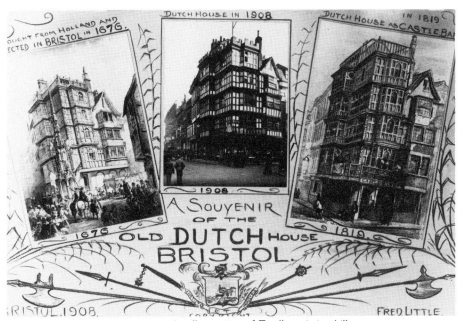

THE HISTORY OF THE DUTCH HOUSE. An illustration of Fred's artistic skills.

THE DUTCH HOUSE at the junction of Wine Street and High Street. Built in 1676 for a wealthy merchant.

THE DUTCH HOUSE which became the Castle Bank in 1810 and Stuckeys Bank in 1826. In 1855 the premises were taken over by T.W. Tilley, a tea merchant.

THE DUTCH HOUSE, taken from Broad Street.

THE DUTCH HOUSE.

ALL SAINTS LANE. All Saints Church in the background is surrounded by buildings so that the south nave aisle is a priest room and over the north is a Georgian Coffee Shop.

ST NICHOLAS MARKET. St Nicholas Church in the background with the Old City Wall forming the south side.

FLOWER MARKET. The frontage was built by Samuel Glascodine with John Wood the Elder in 1745.

THE CORN EXCHANGE of 1743 dominates Corn Street, flanked by the Four Nails. These dish-shaped brass tables were used by merchants to complete their transactions – hence the saying 'pay on the nail'.

CORN STREET. Looking along Corn Street with the Exchange on the left and St Werburgh's Church in the background.

THE FATAL FIRE, 22 August 1910, Lower Maudlin Street. Albert Westlake, aged 45, a general dealer at 8 Lower Maudlin Street, was killed in this fire which started in the early hours of the morning when he and his brother were asleep in their living accommodation above the premises.

THE AFTERMATH OF THE FIRE.

BRISTOL FIRE, Fairfax Street. Fire broke out in the early afternoon on Wednesday, 16 July 1913 in a warehouse used by N. Morley & Sons, dealing in paper and woollen manufacturers' materials. The outbreak occurred at the rear of the premises in a corner of the second floor on the Broadmead side of the brick building. The fire brigade and the Superintendent in charge of the central brigade were quickly on the scene, with the steamer and chemical engine. The firemen experienced some difficulty in getting at the centre of the fire owing to the situation of adjacent buildings, but overcame this by running a hose over the neighbouring premises of John Hall & Sons. By 6 o'clock, the brigade had the fire in hand and no one was seriously hurt.

BRISTOL FIRE, COLSTON STREET. Hoses in action. On the 1 September 1898 fire broke out in Clarke's factory and spread to the adjoining Colston Hall.

CROWDS gather to watch the devastation.

A WAREHOUSE ON FIRE seen from Bristol Bridge.

THE ARMY SERVICE CORPS.

THE ARMY SERVICE CORPS.

THE ROYAL PAVILION.

THE ROYAL PAVILION.

A FINE EXAMPLE OF ANTIQUE BRISTOL GLASS.

ANTIQUE GLASS.

141

GRAPES. Fred enjoyed taking 'still life', as you can see from this superb photograph.

PEAS. Another fine example of Fred's photography.

WALTON CASTLE. The remains of this fine castle at Walton St Mary.

A LOVELY COUNTRY CHURCH IN CLEVEDON.

BOER WAR CANNON. This huge cannon is pictured outside St George's School.

HENBURY CHURCH.

COOKS FOLLY, SNEYD PARK. A youth was locked in the tower for a year but failed to escape a gypsy's threat of imminent death. Built in 1693, the upper tower was removed in 1932 for safety.

HENBURY COTTAGES — Blaise Hamlet. A mock village designed by John Nash for the workers on the Harford Estate.

HENBURY COTTAGES. The cottages are all built around the village green with the village pump in the centre.

HENBURY COTTAGES. Each cottage was a different design, some having thatched roofs and some tiled.

HENBURY COTTAGES. Dial Cottage is on the left with three shafts to the chimney.

ST GEORGES PARK.

EASTVILLE PARK.

THE SNUFF MILL, Frome Glen.

FROME GLEN. One of the many lovely waterfalls that graced the glen.

THE OLD FILE MILL at Winterbourn.

ST ANDREWS PARK. A lovely setting for a Sunday afternoon stroll.

BRISLINGTON. A view across the meadows to the hamlet of Brislington.

AN IDYLLIC SETTING for the village duck pond.

FRED LOVED RECORDING COUNTRY LIFE. These pictures of the sheep sheltering under the trees are a fine example.

A TYPICAL SNOWSCAPE by Fred.

IT IS LOVELY TO SEE THE WILD FOXGLOVES IN THE WOODLAND!

AN OLD RAMSHACKLE MILL with a thatched roof.

LOVERS' MEETING PLACE. The Old File Mill, Winterbourne.

TREE FELLING IN LEIGH WOODS at the top of Rownham Hill.

THE MERMAID who, according to the photographer, was captured at Rownham Ferry at Hotwells in November 1875. She was supposedly washed up the River Avon with the floods which resulted after heavy storms and gales in the area.

ACKNOWLEDGEMENTS

The authors particularly wish to thank Siobhan Murphy, Nigel Moorcroft, Jean Smith and Ernest Wood for their help with the research of this book.

We also acknowledge with much gratitude the help we have received from the Bristol Reference Library and the staff of The Red Lodge.